the
Practical
Meditation
Journal

the
PRACTICAL
Meditation
Journal

Daily Meditations &
Prompts *to* Find Calm
in Everyday Chaos

JIM MARTIN

ROCKRIDGE
PRESS

For general information on our other products and services or to obtain technical support, please contact our Customer Care Department within the United States at (866) 744-2665, or outside the United States at (510) 253-0500.

Rockridge Press publishes its books in a variety of electronic and print formats. Some content that appears in print may not be available in electronic books, and vice versa.

Interior and Cover Designer: John Calmeyer
Art Producer: Sue Bischofberger
Editor: Britt Bogan
Production Manager: Riley Hoffman
Production Editor: Claire Yee

Photography: © Ivan Bandura/Unsplash, pp. viii–1; © Noah Usry/Unsplash, p. 2; © MILKOVÍ/ Unsplash, pp. 14–15; © Ishan @seefromthesky/ Unsplash, pp. 60–61; © Hakan Yalcin/Unsplash, pp. 106–107.

ISBN: Print 978-1-64152-839-9

~~~

This book is dedicated to my wife, Bri.
Without her love, patience, and acceptance,
the life lessons and soul searching that led
to my unique outlook wouldn't have been possible.
I'd also like to dedicate this to my children.
This book is a result of many long hours and
sleepless nights, but I want them to know that you
can overcome anything through hard work.

Meditations

PART ONE

Getting Started

Time for Meditation to Get a Little Unusual

To some people, meditation brings to mind images of monks with shaved heads, robes, and incense in a far-off monastery. Just like most stereotypes, that one misses the mark. (The only reason I shave my head is because of baldness. Sadly, meditation hasn't helped with that.) I have been a meditator for more than 10 years. I have sat in meditation with anger, both physical and mental pain, emotional trauma, and loss. I have also meditated with joy, happiness, and pleasure, and in good times. I am not a monk, nor am I ordained in any school or tradition. To me, meditation is a tool with a purpose, and it is as practical as a hammer. Meditation, simply put, is the act of applying your mind to focus on a given object or thought and holding your awareness there.

For the last eight years, I have dedicated every spare minute to talking and writing about meditation in ways to which normal people can relate, so they can apply meditation to their lives—their real lives. This effort has resulted in massive amounts of content on social media, a podcast, and my site TheUnusualBuddha.com, all of which are dedicated to spreading awareness and breaking down the barriers between real people and a really helpful practice. My whole life has been spent surrounded by practical, pragmatic people, who, on more than one occasion, called me a hippie at the mention of meditation. But almost everyone can meditate, and doing so can help you in your day-to-day life. This journal exists because I wanted to create a tool that I could share with the world—and especially with those who aren't interested in the "love and light" that some practitioners bring to this. Meditation is as practical as dieting for physical health, so read up, follow along, and let's get started!

If you've spent any time looking into meditation online, you'll have noticed there are many different takes on it. Many teachers take a similar New Age approach, involving crystals, spirits, and incense. There is nothing wrong with that approach, but it just doesn't apply to everyone. You don't have to burn sage in dedication to the elders, dance under the moonlight, or enter a monastery to study and wash the feet of a master—unless you're into that sort of thing (no judgment here, just saying…). For some people, this ethereal, metaphysical approach is off-putting and may seem impractical. Why? Because it feels unreal and like there's no substance, nothing to our everyday concerns. Without substance or actually understanding how to apply this tool to your own problems and lifestyle, you're quite frankly ill prepared. Meditation needs to become something natural to you, so much so that you can do it without thinking. You will be able to default to the techniques you've learned here. For many of us, there needs to be a meditation guide more focused on the real world and less on the "woo."

For meditation to stick with you, you'll need to continuously apply yourself to the practice in a way that makes sense to you. Fair weather or not, you'll have to dig in and do the work.

This journal was created to help you regularly practice meditation techniques that can be incorporated into your lifestyle and belief system. Nothing is written here to convert you, there are no tests, and you aren't being graded or judged on your practice—that kind of pressure would be counterproductive and the opposite of what we're after. This journal will help you get into the habit of meditating regularly and give you some real-life, practical meditation methods to apply in scenarios you may commonly face. Plus, it will be a great way to track your journey and see how far you've come.

Unless this book belongs to someone else, write all over the thing, dog-ear the pages, highlight passages—whatever it takes to make the book yours. Keep learning from it and apply what you're learning to the very real-life situations you find yourself in. If one meditation seems difficult or you think you have more work to do there, repeat the session. This book is about growth, not plowing through the material. Working through them at your own speed will lay some serious groundwork for your practice and will give you perspective should the way get a little fuzzy.

Before we dive into the "how," let's take a look at the "why."

Meditation—But Why Though?

Meditation doesn't have to be an over-the-top, "spacey" program dedicated to astral projection. It has serious benefits, including decreasing perceived stress, increasing mental balance, quieting your mind, and achieving sharper focus. Meditation will not lessen your bills or the demands on your time, but it will help you manage the stress and anxiety you feel because of your responsibilities. You'll be better equipped to handle the sense of panic, and in turn, your mood will improve. Your ability to focus and find calm will also improve. You won't find it as hard to quiet the mental chatter in your head. You know what I mean—the inner dialogue that never really seems to quiet down. Depending on your temperament, you may actually be able to control and use the mental chatter to better experience the present moment. You also may notice your relationships becoming stronger because you can spot and peel away layers of nonsense that often impact interactions. When you start to see things with less embellishment, you will tend to gravitate toward other people who are similar to you. In addition, you'll find that you have less tendency to judge yourself and other people, and more inclination toward empathy and compassion. You'll be more grounded in reality and more dedicated to experiencing that reality, especially once you ditch the autopilot behavior that people can fall into. Being present in the moment to genuinely experience what you are living is a true superpower. You'll find that your mood and emotional state are more in balance. Additionally, you'll develop a greater degree of patience. Some people who meditate may even notice improvement in their creativity and their problem-solving abilities. The greatest benefit I have personally found from meditation is the ability to sleep more easily. For those of you who have experienced insomnia, usually it is due to your mood, your emotional state, or a relationship being out of whack. So, although meditation may not directly solve any of your issues, the practice of it may help you in many ways.

Obviously, your individual results from meditation may vary. If you want to dedicate yourself to a particular practice, do it for the sake of that practice and not for gain. If you approach meditation with a "type A" attitude, the learning process may become confusing. There are no achievements here. There is no success or failure. Don't go looking for the Hall of Fame or the Championship Belt of meditation. Just sit and pay attention to your thoughts for the sake of the practice. The benefits of meditation will come in their own time; right now, you need to learn the ropes of meditation.

Don't Sweat the Time

Too many people see meditation as an excessive and wasteful use of time. They believe meditation requires hours or days of them contemplating the mysteries of the universe. The reality is that meditating for even as little as 5 or 10 minutes a day can help you. You can meditate on your commute, while you are in line at the bank, or even when you're warming food in the microwave. You can take as little or as much time as you like to practice, and you will discover, to paraphrase Glinda, the Good Witch from *The Wizard of Oz*, that you've always had the power, you just had to discover that power yourself.

If you dedicate yourself to developing mindfulness, that is, staying focused and remaining aware of the present moment, and you learn to incorporate mindfulness into your daily routine, then every minute becomes part of your practice. Every breath and every step you take, every dish you wash, every trivial task you perform becomes the practice without distracting from the task itself. In fact, you may find that your daily activities no longer seem mundane when they become part of your mindfulness path.

You can also dedicate a little daily time to a more formal style of practice, during which you sit comfortably on the floor or in a straight-backed chair and quietly allow your awareness to stretch out in front of you. I personally like a hybrid of the two methods described here: the more relaxed on-the-go practice combined with the formal seated practice, using the most fitting style for a given situation. If you are just beginning to meditate, try some kind of meditation once a day for a solid week, at different times, so you can find what form works best for you. Just like planting an apple seed will yield an apple tree, in meditation you have to set up the right environment to get the desired result.

How to Meditate, Simply Put

Now we're getting into the good stuff—how to actually meditate.

PICKING A PLACE

Find a decently quiet place to meditate. This doesn't mean the place has to be as silent as a library. Just don't try meditation at a concert, at least not at first. Look for a comfortable place that is safe and reasonably free of distractions.

If you would prefer to meditate in the seated style, here are a few pointers for staying comfortable and getting the most out of the practice. First, elevate your bottom: Ideally, your hips should be slightly higher than your knees. I roll up a regular sleeping pillow to sit on. Play around with things like towels, blankets, or cushions. Start with materials you have on hand. Some of the seats, like zafu or zabuton meditation cushions, can get pricey, and at the end of the day, they're still just seats.

Some people like to sit with their legs crossed comfortably, or "crisscross applesauce," as teachers tell kindergarteners. If you are a glutton for punishment, you could attempt to sit in the lotus position (for MMA fans, that's the equivalent of a self-inflicted heel hook—YouTube that move, it's brutal). You're welcome to attempt the lotus position, but just know that it can be tough. Some folks even prefer to meditate lying down. Some others lie on their right side. Take whatever position floats your boat, but position yourself so you're comfortable.

If you choose to meditate in a chair, pick one with a straight back. This type of chair will set you up for success by giving you the support you need if and when you nod off. Meditating in a chair is ideal for people who have chronic knee, hip, or back pain. The practice is equally effective whether you are sitting in a chair or on the floor. The mind work is the most important thing in meditation, so don't place too much emphasis on how you are seated.

Once you have the seat situation set up to your liking, a little stretching may be in order. Elevating your bottom and stretching are all about saving you some back pain. Once you are seated and loosened up, place your hands in a position of comfort. Some people like to place their hands with the palms down on their thighs, some choose to place their hands palms up, and others gently place their hands in their lap. Feel free to experiment. Just as with your seating position, the mind work is much more important than the exact placement of the hands.

TIMERS ARE YOUR FRIEND

Using a timer will allow you to invest yourself in the practice without worrying about missing anything. Any time-keeping device can be used as long as there is a chime function in it. There are many apps and timers to use. My personal favorite timekeeper is Meditation Assistant from Rocket Nine Laboratories. This free app keeps track of sessions and series of sessions. Although I don't suggest getting into a competitive mind-set with your practice, it can be helpful to track trends in your moments of meditation. At first, you'll feel every millisecond of practice, so the minutes will crawl by. The timer will keep you on track. Start at five minutes and work your way up to longer sessions from there.

DOING THE THING

There are many different ways to meditate. The basic idea is to stay mentally focused on the object of your meditation, which can change based on your intentions and needs for the day. The type of meditation that works for you may not work for me, and vice versa. Don't get judgmental with yourself. When you lose the object of your focus, just gently come back to that object. Even if your time focusing on the object is brief, that's okay—keep doing the exercise. Just be patient and give meditation a fair shot. You'll be surprised at what may come from practicing it.

EXPERIMENTATION IS GOOD

Just like any habit you begin, make this practice your own. Try different positions and different times of day. Try meditating for 5, 10, or 30 minutes a day. Or meditate with no set minutes. You can use a timer that simply documents the end of the session when you stop the clock. The point of experimenting is to try to find what form of meditation works for you. At the end of the day, this is your practice; don't stress about doing it. Just keep coming back to meditation—it gets better.

How to Use This Journal

In the following sections, you'll be presented with different meditations, each with a description outlining the exercise and a time recommendation to spend on it. The recommendations will be 5, 10, or 30 minutes, getting longer as you gain experience; however, the exact time you choose is up to you. Sit with it as long as you can. Choose the amount of time and the posture that best suit you and your setting. If one day requires sitting on a cushion or chair, great; if the next day requires a walking meditation, fantastic. Mix up your meditations in whatever way you feel comfortable. If a meditation isn't quite something you can do for any reason, such as a walking meditation if walking is difficult for you on some days, feel free to do the meditation however you can, such as sitting and feeling some grass instead.

In the reflection sections, you'll note where each meditation took you or what you experienced. Record what came to mind during the session. Take a minute to really reflect here. This reflection is about your growth, not about writing. So, jot down as much or as little information as you like. The reflection sections are a place to make sure you are getting the most out of each session.

After each meditation and reflection, you'll be asked to set a daily intention to guide you as you go about your day. The intention you choose is entirely up to you, but you'll be given a suggestion should nothing come to mind. Consider intentions such as "Today, I will take a brief walk at lunch, meditate twice, etc." These mini-goals don't have to be earth-shattering. Just decide on a goal that relates to meditation, mindfulness, or self-care.

Finally, there are prompts based on each meditation. The prompts are intended to help add depth to your practice. There will be lists, journaling, and maybe even a picture or two to draw. These features may sound a little intimidating, but creating a journal is really one of the best ways to build a meditation practice that is deep and effective. If an activity gets uncomfortable, skip it and come back to it later when you're in a better place to deal with it.

The idea of this journal is to read the meditation of the day, carry out the session, write your reflection of the session, set your intention, carry out the intention throughout the day, and then write your response to the prompt. Remember, this journal is for you. If you have to alter the structure of an activity, feel free to do that. This is a practical guide, not a strict prescription. I want you to grab the practice of meditation by the horns and own it in a way that is uniquely yours. In fact, the more unusual your practice, the better!

Breathe Out the Bad; Breathe In the Good

In the space provided, write all the negative aspects that come to mind when you think of meditation.

What factors bring you to meditation? Use the space provided to describe your reasons in as much detail as possible.

PART TWO

Meditations

There are 22 meditations in this journal that you'll cycle through three times. Each iteration will seek to dig a little deeper and be a little longer than the last. The first iteration should be a bit easy so you can focus on familiarizing yourself with the practices covered. You can go through the book in order or skip around in any way you wish.

Body Scan, Waking

As you wake up, lie in bed and try to experience the sensations of your body on the bed. Scan your body, starting at the bottom of your feet, and slowly work your way up to your ankles and calves, knees and thighs. Continue on to your hips and abdomen. Next, focus on your chest and arms, and then your neck and head. What is it like to become fully aware of each part of your body, one part at a time? Are some parts of your body partially asleep? Do some feel heavy? Does your blanket feel warm against your chest, but does your foot feel cold because it is poking out from under the blanket? Run through this cycle a couple times to thoroughly experience each sensation and each part of your body. Practice this meditation for 5 minutes.

REFLECTION

Use the lines provided to note the sensations that came to mind as you scanned your body.

Today, set an intention that will help you "turn off the autopilot" and actually experience what it feels like to be in your own skin. *Example: Today, I will consciously experience my touch sensation, and be truly aware of my body and its sensations.*

Most of us will live into our eighties or beyond, but we are only fully aware of a small percentage of that time. How often do you mindfully experience your day versus just coasting past the experiences you've been afforded?

Body Scan, Midday

This meditation is a midday body scan. Take care of your own needs at this point of the day. Use the restroom, eat lunch, hydrate, and so on. Once you have taken care of all those things, find a comfortable position: sitting, standing, walking, or whatever floats your boat. Now that you've moved through the morning funk that most of us experience, perform a body scan. Slowly, going from head to toe, focus on experiencing every part of your body in as much depth as you're able to. Take your time and experience each inch of your head, face, neck, shoulders, arms, chest—moving all the way down to your toes. Spend 5 minutes practicing this meditation.

REFLECTION

Once you've completed the session, reflect on your experience in the space provided.

INTENTION

Today, I will monitor my body and its sensations. I will do something good for my body, like eat a healthy lunch or take the stairs instead of the elevator.

In the space provided, write one thing you've discovered about your body in this practice. Are you making your migraines worse by the way you clench your teeth, or does the way you hold your shoulders lead you to tension headaches?

Body Scan, Bedtime

Now that the day is complete and you're ready for bed, you're going to perform a body scan. Lie down in a position of comfort. Close your eyes and feel your whole body, from head to toe. Let go of the baggage you've taken on from the day. Relax your shoulders, unclench your jaw, breathe, and relax. Let work live at work and let yourself rest. Start this practice about 5 minutes before your bedtime.

REFLECTION

Using the space provided, reflect on your experience as you truly leave work at work.

INTENTION

Today, I will not bring work home with me. I will allow myself to truly decompress after the day's tasks are done, and I will feel what the stressors of the day do to my body.

Write the first thing that comes to mind and a brief explanation of why when you think of each term:

Work

Stress

Deadlines

Supervisors

Responsibilities

Time management

Mindful Commute

Ruminate on this meditation when you are doing an activity, but also leave space to focus on the way your body feels as you ride the bus, go for a run, or commute to work. Tune in to the white noise-like sensation of bus-riding, running, or driving, using all your senses (excluding taste). How do you experience the way the bus rumbles? How much give does the surface you're running on have? What does your car's steering wheel feel like in your hands? Aim to notice what you've been missing during these activities. Practice this meditation for 5 minutes.

REFLECTION

Use this space to reflect on this mindful traveling session. What was this session like? How did it make you feel?

INTENTION

Today, you'll center your intention on the overlooked sense experiences within your everyday tasks. *Example: Today, I will keep my focus on one sense—sight, sound, touch, taste, or smell. I will notice what my morning coffee actually smells like, listen to the sounds present in my workplace, etc.*

Using your senses is a huge factor in a mindfulness meditation practice. List some things you noticed while applying this technique;
pick one or all of those things you noticed, and fill out each category
with details as thoroughly as you can.

Sight

Sound

Touch

Smell

Cause and Effect Meditation, Anger

How many times do you find yourself just reacting to someone in anger? In this meditation, think of a time when you reacted from a negative place. The more recent the event, the better for this practice. Starting at the moment you "blew up," think in reverse order and determine what mental event immediately preceded that blowup. When you have identified it, determine what mental event preceded that other mental event. Trace each moment in reverse order as far back as you can. Obviously, this will take some time, so be patient. This practice will eventually bring you to places in your mind that may still be a bit tender. These triggers begin to ease their stranglehold when brought into the light. Keep at this practice and remember to be gentle. This meditation is heavier than most other ones. Practice this meditation for 5 minutes.

REFLECTION

Using the space provided, outline your experience.

Today, set an intention that will require you to pay closer attention to your actions and reactions. *Example: Today, I will pause and take a breath before I react. If I do have a snap reaction today, I will trace the causes as far back as I can in order to find the initial cause.*

In the space provided, list the five most common causes of your anger-filled responses and what usually precedes your response.

Finding Impermanence in the Minute Details

Here's a meditation for coffee and tea lovers. Prep your coffee, tea, or cocoa as you always do, but this time observe the impermanent loops and curls the creamer or milk creates as you pour it into your beverage. If you don't use creamer, take this time to rethink your life choices (kidding!). Observe the sugar as it dissolves into the hot liquid. Take this as a sign to be more fluid today and to go with the flow, mindfully observing even the smallest things. Spend 5 minutes on this meditation.

REFLECTION

After watching this tiny phenomenon of miniscule changes in your beverage, reflect upon the flow of life as a whole. Just as water flows to its destination, allow your awareness to flow. Use the space provided to reflect on the flow of your awareness.

INTENTION

Focus today's intention on liquid and flow. *Example: Today, I will hydrate myself well or find three examples of flow (water, traffic, lunchroom foot traffic, etc.—get creative).*

In the space provided, list 10 ways in which you feel you may be too rigid.

Walking Meditation

You've probably already done something like this walking meditation on multiple occasions. This time, take a walk and focus on the sensation of your feet touching the ground. Actively pay attention to the sensation of one foot pressing into the ground, so the other may be gently and mindfully placed. As you do this action, mentally note "left, right, left, right." This meditation will help keep you centered in the task. The more senses you can tie in to this experience, the more lasting and fulfilling the practice will become. So, if you can, try to do this exercise barefoot. Aim to practice this meditation for 5 minutes.

REFLECTION

In the space provided, write about your experience performing a simple walking meditation.

INTENTION

Today's intention will center on walking. *Example: Today, I will skip the elevator or escalator and take the stairs, making sure to experience every step I take.*

Use the space provided to note where your attention is drawn while you are trying to practice this meditation. Be honest; you'll be the only one reading this journal. Are you thinking about dinner, home life, work, third grade? List the things that are trying to claim your attention.

Contentment Meditation

In this session, you will meditate on good times; these good occasions have lessons to teach you. Focus on a time you were really happy, and I mean more than happy—I mean content. And by content, I mean happy in the most simplistic terms, such as being pleased by your minimum needs being met. Focus your mind right there on that sensation. Explore the borders of it: witness or experience the object of your meditation so keenly that the subject and object are nearly indiscernible. Practice this meditation for 5 minutes.

REFLECTION

In the space provided, write about your experience exploring your contented mind.

INTENTION

Focus today's intention on something that makes you happy.
Example: Today, I will do something that makes me happy. I will be fully aware of each moment of this experience.

List 10 things that make you happy and write down the first thought that comes to mind when you think of each. If summer makes you happy, what is the first thing that comes to mind when you think of summer? For example, fresh-cut grass, hot weather, etc.

Serenity Meditation

This style of meditation is commonly called a serenity meditation. You can do this meditation at work or before your daily tasks. Specifically, do this exercise before you're on the clock. Sit in a straight-backed chair or on the floor (you can even do this in your car; whatever position you find comfortable and that fits your surroundings). Close your eyes and focus on exactly where you feel the breathing sensation. Some people focus on the tip of the nose, some people focus on the rise and fall of their chest, and some lucky few feel their breath grazing their amazingly groomed mustache (or maybe that's just me . . .). Whatever you feel, keep your awareness there. Do this meditation for at least 5 minutes, or more if you can.

REFLECTION

Use the space provided to put your experience with the serenity meditation into words. Be as descriptive as you possibly can.

Today, you will center your intention on feeling the breathing sensation. *Example: Today, I will focus on where in my body I most strongly feel the breathing sensation. I will take note of my breath before reacting. I will mentally note the "in and out" of my breathing.*

In the space provided, in as much detail as possible, write where in your body you feel the sensation of breathing.

Gratitude Meditation

This meditation is centered on gratitude. No matter how humbly you live or how little you possess, there is always something to inspire gratitude. Today, you're going to focus on things you are grateful for. You can sit, walk, lie down, or stand—whatever is most comfortable for you. Focus on what you are grateful for, other than possessions: health, friendship, contentment, or whatever comes to mind when you ask yourself "What am I grateful for?" Practice this meditation for 5 minutes.

In the space provided, reflect on how an attitude of gratitude feels. How could you benefit from spending more time focusing on gratitude?

Today's intention will be about noticing all the little things you should be grateful for but usually overlook. *Example: Today, I will consider how amazing it is to have running water, or I will appreciate an opportunity to learn something new.*

In the lines provided below, list all the things that make you feel grateful.

Loving-Kindness Meditation, Self

This style of meditation is called loving-kindness. It is simple yet very edifying in terms of personal happiness. This practice can stave off the aloofness that some of the other techniques can bring. Find a place you can sit, lie, or stand comfortably. Then, picture yourself safe, happy, healthy, content, and loved. When you get a warm and fuzzy feeling from these images, hold onto it. Feeling safe, happy, healthy, content, and loved are things most people search for in life. Whether someone admits it or not, most people have a certain degree of negative self-image issues that prevent us from feeling good about ourselves. This practice will change those negative thoughts! Practice this meditation for at least 5 minutes.

REFLECTION

Once you've practiced this visualization for at least 5 minutes, write about your experience in the space provided.

Today's intention will center on your self-image. *Example: Today, I will recognize when I engage in negative self-image talk and inner dialogue. I will redirect internal negativity with a positive spin. Don't say "I am so stupid," but instead think, "I need to slow down so I don't miss things."*

In the space provided, write the most common mental phrases you use in which you cut yourself down. What negative things come up in your internal dialogue?

Loving-Kindness Meditation, Neutral One

In the "self" session of loving-kindness that came before this one, you generated good feelings toward yourself. Start this "neutral" session in exactly the same way, by generating warm feelings. Then, transfer those feelings over to someone you are neutral toward. Lost? I'll explain. We all have people we cross paths with, sometimes on a regular basis, whom we politely smile at and then disregard. In this meditation, the people you would normally treat with mild neglect will now be the target of your generated sensations of happiness, safety, contentment, love, etc. Build the good feelings you want for yourself, and then project them onto these other "neutral" people. Allow at least 5 minutes for this practice to simmer, but feel free to do the meditation as long as you like.

REFLECTION

Once you have completed this session, use the space provided to reflect on your experience generating positive feelings and transferring them to someone you would usually pay no mind to.

Today's intention will center on the people you often barely acknowledge. *Example: Today, I will genuinely smile at a stranger at the gas pump or grocery store. I will consider what a stranger's "story" might be as I pass by them.*

In the space provided, write about a person you see repeatedly but don't usually engage with. What are they like? How often do you see them? Do they seem happy? Consider them and write what comes to mind about them.

Loving-Kindness Meditation, Difficult One

This final session of loving-kindness is a doozy. Start the meditation like you did in the first session, by picturing yourself safe, happy, healthy, content, and loved. When you reach that mind-set, move those feelings onto someone you don't like. The more you dislike the person you are thinking of, the better, because this exercise will require you to engage in some real personal growth and to mentally take the high road. The practice is taxing, but the juice here is worth the squeeze! Do this meditation for a minimum of 5 minutes, but feel free to continue the practice as long as your time and temperament allow. Feel free to repeat this session if necessary.

REFLECTION

Once you've completed this intense session, you may find that repeating the meditation a few more times will really drive the point of it home. In the space provided, write all that comes to mind about your experience wishing well on someone who you think might not deserve the positive thoughts.

Today's intention will center on the grudges you hold.

Example: Today, I will examine the grudges I am holding on to; I will acknowledge how long I have been holding on to these grudges.

Whether a person "deserves" you to hold a grudge against them isn't the point. How many grudges are you holding on to? How long have you been holding on to them? Who is being punished by your holding these grudges? Please note that letting go of a grudge toward someone does not mean you have to invite that person back into your life. Think of releasing the grudge against someone as evicting that person from the space they have been occupying, rent-free, in your mind. You are taking back control of your emotions!

PROMPT

In keeping with the grudge theme, in the space provided, write about a grudge you still hold. Think of the biggest grudge you hold, what started it, and how long you have held on to it. Will letting go of the grudge ease the emotional weight from your shoulders?

Observing the Mind Meditation

This meditation centers on the mind more than all the other meditations. In this one, the mind itself will be the object we watch. As much as you can, in general, pay attention to your mind throughout the whole day. Where does it go in the thought process? How long does it stay on those thoughts? What thoughts do you normally have? Where do those thoughts lead you? Try to stay with this meditation all day. If you find you've stopped meditating, it's okay, gently get back into the zone. Practice this meditation for at least 5 minutes.

REFLECTION

Once you've maintained this practice for as long as you can in a day, reflect on your experience in the space provided.

INTENTION

Today, I will carefully note where my mind goes all day. I will quietly observe my mind with no judgment.

In the space provided, list five things you like about where your mind tracks regularly. Then, write five things that your mind tracks that you want to change.

Random Act of Kindness, Meditation

This meditation will center on a kind act you have performed. If you can't think of a kind act you've done recently, go do one and come back to this. Now that you have a fresh act of kindness under your belt, use mindfulness to fully experience the sensation you have from carrying out this act. Where are the "edges" of this sensation? For example, focus on knowing this sensation so intimately that you can clearly tell where your experience of it begins and ends. How does the feeling you get from doing something kind for someone else differ from the happiness you feel about good fortune in your own life? Focus on this experience for 5 minutes.

REFLECTION

Using the space provided, write about your experience performing an act of kindness.

INTENTION

Today, I will do something kind for someone and expect nothing in return, and I will look for a small act of kindness another person has done for someone else.

In the space provided, list one kind thing you can do for a different person every day of the next week.

Emptiness Meditation

In this session, we will meditate on emptiness. Question: What makes a cup most useful? Answer: the fact that it's empty makes the cup the most usable and useful. In this meditation, observe your mind in situations when you had to learn a skill from another person. Do you feel internal resistance? Why does this resistance exist? Where does it come from? Practice this meditation for 5 minutes.

In the space provided, reflect on the usefulness of coming to a learning experience with an "empty cup."

Today, I will learn a new skill, no matter how small, and observe the process as objectively as I can.

In the space provided, write about a time when you and the "I already know" mentality affected a learning experience.

Mantra Meditation

Now that you're this far into the journal, let's get a little weird. This session will be a mantra meditation practice. Traditionally, this meditation is done with some kind of Sanskrit phrase. I can assure you such a phrase isn't necessary, but for simplicity's sake we'll use "Om," which is easy to repeat and we can say it with some serious decibels. Find a place where you won't disturb anyone. With the most emphasis on making the word vibrate in the throat, repeat the word "Om." The tone should land somewhere between a note and a scream. Usually, people who practice this regularly will get a *mala*, which is a string of 108 beads that meditators use for counting, by passing the beads through the fingers. Aim to practice this meditation for 5 minutes.

REFLECTION

After your session, write about your experience in the space provided.

INTENTION

Today, I will dedicate mindfulness to what I say, both internally and aloud. I will see how my words and tones affect other people and different situations.

PROMPT
In the space provided, list five negative phrases you say internally or aloud, then list five positive versions of those phrases. *Example: "I'm not smart enough" might become "I will study harder."*

Rise and Fall Meditation

Life consists of a steady cycle of rise and fall. Focus on the rise and fall sensation of your diaphragm as you breathe. Breathe in deeply, let the air fill your lungs, feel your belly expand, then breathe out, letting the air empty from your lungs as your stomach sinks. As I do this meditation, I like to envision a calm day at the beach as the waves come and go gently. Contemplate rise and fall for 5 minutes.

REFLECTION

Reflect on the rise and fall sensation in the space provided.

INTENTION

Today, focus on observing transitions. For example, the change from day to night, the shift in your mood as a day goes on, etc.

Write about a time of transition in your life—one in which you experienced a change from one polar opposite to another.

Mental "Quiet Space" Meditation

In this meditation, you will look at the mind and its processes. Practice this meditation in the position in which you are the most comfortable. Once you get settled, begin to watch your mind and its thoughts. Don't invest in any of the thoughts. Instead think of them as slideshows—images scrolling by you, the observer. Now for the fun part: Focus on the little space "between" the slides. Thoughts will continue to come and go, but your home base is going to be in between the thoughts. This "in between" moment may be milliseconds or could go on for hours. Track the spaces between thoughts for as long as you can. Practice this meditation for at least 5 minutes.

REFLECTION

In the space provided, write about your experience expanding the quiet space between thoughts.

INTENTION

Today, I will observe the sheer volume of visually based thoughts I have as I go through the day, appreciate the space between my thoughts, and notice when the mental chatter is down to a dull roar.

In the blank space provided, draw a representation of how thoughts flow through your mind. Do they play out like a film? Do you experience the thoughts as though you were sitting at a train crossing and each train car is another idea? How do the thoughts move through your mind?

Sadness Meditation

In this meditation, you will observe your mind in a moment of sadness. Think of a time that caused you sadness. What was your mind like in that sad state? Did you deal with the source of the sadness or repress the feeling as some people do? Did thinking of that event bring those pangs of sadness? Think of a time of sadness in your life and observe how you mentally moved through it. Meditate on this experience for 5 minutes.

REFLECTION

Write about your experience in this session in the space provided.

INTENTION

Today, I will gain better understanding of how I process bad news, observe my relationship with sadness, and face my emotional issues.

In the space provided, recount a moment of sadness from your life and how you handled the emotion. Did you face it, bury it, or escape it? Did you handle the situation well? In what ways can you change how you process sadness?

All-Sense Input Meditation

This meditation is a mindfulness practice with a focus on all experienced sensations. As you go through your day, mentally note every quantifiable experience you can, as they occur, from the grossest to the subtlest. When you breathe, think "in and out," and when you walk, think "left, right, left, right." When thoughts appear, simply note, "thinking," and so on. Don't attach yourself to the notes, just call out the note mentally and move on. This will be a whole day's practice. Practice this meditation for at least 5 minutes.

Reflect on your experience of this session in the space provided.

Today, I will challenge myself to actively experience this whole day, appreciate how much time is gained while I'm off of "autopilot," and note the experience of the most subtle mental or physical phenomenon I can find within myself.

In the space provided, describe, in as great detail as possible, one seemingly mundane experience you have had.

Eating Meditation

This meditation will be done over a meal. You are going to mindfully eat this meal, so prepare the meal, making sure all appropriate internal temperatures are reached. Once you sit down to eat, look at the meal. What does it look like? What colors do you see in it? How is it plated? Next, what does it smell like? Put some food on your fork. What does the food feel like? (Don't use this as an excuse to dunk your hands into Grandma's potato salad.) Take a bite. How does the food feel in your mouth? Is it crunchy, al dente, chewy, or creamy? As you chew, notice how the food tastes. Is it sweet, salty, or savory? Thoroughly chew that bite and swallow. Practice this meditation for at least 5 minutes.

REFLECTION

Write about your experience with this session in the space provided.

INTENTION

Today, I will make better food choices; make more sensible portion decisions; and eat when I'm hungry, not because I'm bored.

In the space provided, list what sensations you notice as you eat your favorite meal.

Sight

Sound (if applicable, such as sizzling)

Smell

Touch

Taste

Bonus: What experiences does this meal bring to mind?

If you have followed this journal page by page, you have completed 22 meditations to get here. Now we'll extend the time you spend on each meditation and turn up the heat a little.

Body Scan, Waking

Now that you have developed some expertise in meditation, an early morning body scan should be a piece of cake. Use your blossoming mindfulness skills upon waking to scan your body from head to toe. Pay attention to the sensations present at each point of your scan. Practice this meditation for 10 minutes.

REFLECTION
In the space provided, write about your experience this session.

INTENTION
Today's intention will center on extending this period of mindfulness throughout the day. You're off to a great start. See how far you can take this practice today. *Example: Today, I will carry out more tasks with mindfulness.*

What is something you are more aware of now that you have been meditating?

Body Scan, Midday

This session will be a midday body scan. At this point, you've made it through the morning shenanigans. Take 10 minutes midday to do a quick body scan. This time try to use your focus to "zoom in" on each body part even tighter, like a microscope switching from 10x to 100x magnification. Start scanning from your feet to your head, and try to feel each muscle and joint as intimately as you can.

REFLECTION

Once you've completed the session, reflect on your experience in the space provided.

INTENTION

Today, I will pay attention to my body. Am I taking care of myself?

Are you taking care of your body? In what ways could you improve your self-care regimen?

Body Scan, Bedtime

In this bedtime body scan, you will focus more closely on your body than you did in the previous bedtime session. While lying in bed, do a body scan. This time, you're looking to go from a focus of 10x to a focus of 100x. Feel every muscle and joint from your feet all the way to your head. Feel where each muscle begins and ends. Practice this meditation for 10 minutes. Set a timer. If you complete the scan before the timer goes off, start again.

REFLECTION

Reflect on this session in the space provided.

INTENTION

Now that the day is done, I will truly "let go" of this day.

What differences do you notice in your body as you perform a body scan before bed?

Mindful Commute

Travel is one of the most frequent periods of quiet time many of us have. As you travel, observe and mentally note all of your sensory experiences. Practice this meditation for 10 minutes.

Use the space provided to reflect on this travel session.

Today, I will take the long way home. A longer trip means more time to meditate.

Number the four senses in the list provided in the order of their prominence in your practice.

Sight

Hearing

Touch

Smell

Anger Meditation

For most of us, anger is an engrossing experience. Think of a time when you were angry, then think of the chain of events that took you from a neutral to an angry mental state. Practice this meditation for 10 minutes.

REFLECTION

Reflect on your experience in the space provided.

INTENTION

Today, I will observe my emotional state.

What are some things that make you angry? Why do they make you angry?

Minute Impermanence

Here's a meditation for the coffee and tea lovers in the crowd. Prep your coffee, tea, or cocoa as you always do, but this time observe the impermanent loops and curls the creamer or milk creates as you pour it into the beverage. Consider the phenomenon of impermanence. Meditate on impermanence for 10 minutes.

Reflect on your experience meditating on impermanence.

Today, I will look for instances of impermanence and the changes in fortune impermanence can bring me.

Write about a time when impermanence was made most clear to you.

Walking Meditation

This session is a walking meditation. Rather than letting your mind wander, you are going to focus on the sensations you experience. In the last walking meditation, you mentally noted "left, right, left" so you could stay with the present moment as you walked. This time you'll mentally add in the sounds of your surroundings. As you move, think, "left, right, listen, left, right, hear," and so forth. Do not pass judgment on anything you notice. Keep your focus in this loop for a full 10-minute session.

REFLECTION

In the space provided, write about your experience performing a deeper walking meditation.

INTENTION

Today, I will take some time to appreciate my growing mindfulness practice.

What sensations are becoming more apparent to you as you practice mindfulness more often?

Contentment Meditation

In this meditation, you will be meditating on good times. Meditate on what you actually need in order to be content: food, shelter, water, clothing, etc. What are your minimum requirements for contentment? Focus on this exercise for 10 minutes.

REFLECTION

In the space provided, write about your experience in exploring the minimalist version of what makes you content.

INTENTION

Focus today's intention on something that makes you happy and why it makes you happy.

What do you need to be happy?

Serenity Meditation

Find a reasonably quiet place where you can sit, stand, or walk. Once you've found the ideal position for your comfort, focus on your breath. Focus on where you feel the breathing sensation the most. For most people, it will be the nose or upper lip area. Be sure to stay focused on that spot—don't follow your breath into your body (your focus will become too body-centered), and don't follow your breath into the room (your focus will be drawn to the room). Just stay at the gateway of the breath and observe the breathing sensation as it comes and goes. Do this meditation for 10 minutes.

REFLECTION

Reflect on your breathing-focused meditation.

INTENTION

Today, I will notice how my breath changes under different circumstances during the day.

In the space provided, in as much detail as possible, write about how your breathing changes under different circumstances.

Gratitude Meditation

Consider whom you are grateful for in your life. Reflect on this person and what behaviors they bring out in you. What traits do they have that make you grateful for them? Practice this meditation for 10 minutes.

Reflect on the positive effect this person has on your life.

Today, I will look for the admirable and valuable qualities I possess.

In the space provided, list the valuable qualities you possess and the qualities you want to work on.

Loving-Kindness Meditation, Self

Find a position of comfort sitting, standing, or walking. Once you are set, envision yourself happy, healthy, safe, and cared for. If it helps, you can even repeat the words, "I am happy, I am healthy, I am safe, I am cared for." This style of meditation is called metta. Focus on the feelings you're generating—they are the goal. Perform this practice for 10 minutes.

REFLECTION

Once you've completed your session, reflect on it briefly in the space provided.

INTENTION

Today, I will do something that makes me happy (preferably, at no one else's expense).

What is your greatest source of happiness?

Loving-Kindness Meditation, Neutral One

Start this round of metta practice the same way you started it in the last session. First, sit, stand, or walk. Once you've found your position of comfort, envision yourself happy, healthy, safe, and cared for. Once you notice a tingle of positive emotions and you know the meditation is working, move those positive feelings to someone you are neutral toward. It can be someone from work or your neighborhood, or distant relatives. Just think of someone you have no strong feelings toward. Move the generated good feelings onto them, and imagine them happy, healthy, safe, and cared for. If it helps with your practice, you can even quietly repeat "May you be happy, may you be healthy, may you be safe, may you be cared for." Practice this meditation for at least 10 minutes.

REFLECTION

Once you have completed this session, use the space provided to reflect on the experience of generating positive feelings and moving them to someone you would usually pay no mind to.

INTENTION

Today, I will make an effort to safely and warmly greet someone I feel neutral toward.

How many people do you think consider you their "neutral one"? Why?

Loving-Kindness Meditation, Difficult One

In this last round of metta, once again find a position of comfort for yourself. Begin to imagine yourself happy, healthy, safe, and cared for. Then, just like last time, when you notice a tingle of positive emotions and you know the meditation is working, swap the intended recipient of your positive thoughts. This time the lucky duck is someone you don't like. Imagine this person happy, healthy, safe, and cared for. As before, if it helps, you can softly repeat the phrase "May you be happy, may you be healthy, may you be safe, may you be cared for." This round of meditation may be tougher than the other rounds and it may take longer to complete. Keep pushing through the exercise. Remember, this practice in no way condones or erases the past actions or behaviors of the person you are contemplating. This meditation is about you releasing a grudge. Practice this meditation for at least 10 minutes.

REFLECTION

Reflect on your experience with this meditation.

INTENTION

Today, I will consider how many grudges I am holding, and how much of the past I am carrying with me every day.

What would your life be like if you carried no grudges whatsoever?

Observing the Mind

In this meditation, you'll be practicing "mindfulness of the mind." That's just a fancy way to say you'll be using your mind to observe your mind. Find a position of comfort sitting, standing, or walking. Carefully observe your mind. Where does it go when it trails? Don't invest too much time thinking about where your mind takes you, just follow the waves of thought. Observe your mind and its ability to rise and fall, that is, the mind's ability to fade in and out of any thought or mental phenomenon. Practice this meditation for at least 10 minutes.

REFLECTION

Reflect on the effects of this practice.

INTENTION

Today, I will objectively observe my mind and where it goes.

Do you control your mind or do you allow it to go where it will?
Why does that particular circumstance happen?

Random Act of Kindness Meditation

In this session, you will focus on performing a kind act and how that action feels. You can carry out a big or small act, that part is not important. Do something for someone else and, for 10 minutes, focus on how doing that kind act makes you feel.

REFLECTION

Once you've thought about this experience for 10 minutes, write your reflections in the space provided.

INTENTION

Today, I will do something kind for someone else and truly take in the experience.

How often do I show kindness to someone from whom I expect nothing? How often do I act selflessly?

Emptiness Meditation

In this session, you will be meditating on emptiness. Consider it the most natural state of your mind. Generally speaking, you are at peace until something moves you from that feeling. In this session, focus on what your mind is doing when you aren't worried about school, work, bills, or any other troublesome things. Practice this meditation for 10 minutes.

REFLECTION

Use the space provided to reflect on this session.

INTENTION

Today, I will focus on the "quiet space" between my thoughts.

When do you feel most at peace?

Mantra Meditation

For this session, pick a mantra or affirmation to repeat. Try to find a judgment-free area where you can meditate, and spend 10 minutes reciting your mantra. Put some power behind your recitation, and focus on the vibrating quality of the sound or sounds you are making. Practice this meditation for 10 minutes.

After your session, write about your experience in the space provided.

Today, I will focus on what I say and how it affects people around me.

Where does your mind go when you try to quiet it?

Rise and Fall Meditation

Life consists of a steady cycle of rise and fall. Focus on the rise and fall sensation of your diaphragm (the muscle in the middle of your chest, just below your rib cage) as you breathe. Remember the belly-breathing technique described earlier in the journal. Fill your whole person with each inhalation and think or repeat "rise and fall" softly to yourself. Practice this meditation for 10 minutes.

REFLECTION

In the space provided, reflect on the rise and fall sensation of your breathing.

INTENTION

Today, I will focus on breathing calmly to proactively change my state of mind.

How is your breathing affected throughout an ordinary day?
Do your emotions affect your breathing?

Mental "Quiet Space" Meditation

In this meditation, you will look at your mind and its processes. Meditate in the position in which you are the most comfortable: sitting, standing, or walking. Observe your mind as you have in the earlier sessions. As soon as an active thought ends, focus on that quiet space, the "space" between mental events. With repeated practice this space will expand. Once it does, you'll feel like you've built an addition onto your mind. Practice this meditation for 10 minutes.

REFLECTION

Write about your experience expanding the space between thoughts.

INTENTION

Today, I will consider and appreciate the "negative spaces," or spaces where there is only openness and emptiness.

Think about ways you are too "closed off" and restricted. These restrictions could be caused by you or an outside influence (work, society, or family). Consider the opportunity for freedom in emptiness and write about a scenario in which you would benefit from a little more freedom that emptiness can provide.

Sadness Meditation

In this meditation, you will observe your mind in a moment of sadness. Sadness can be a very encompassing emotional experience. Using your ever-sharpening awareness, observe your sadness: sit with it, examine it. What caused this emotion? Practice this meditation for 10 minutes.

REFLECTION
Write about your experience of this session in the space provided.

INTENTION
Today, I will examine how I process sadness and come to terms with that emotion.

Consider your moments of sadness. Are they actually as sad as they seem or is there a degree of mental embellishment?

All-Sense Input Meditation

This meditation is a mindfulness practice with a focus on all experienced sensations. Rather than focusing on one specific sensation, use this session to work on broadening your mindfulness scope. Attempt to mentally note all your sense observations. This practice should be done while you carry out your normal daily activities. Practice this meditation in 10-minute intervals.

Reflect on your experience of this session in the space provided.

Today, I will perform a normally mindless activity (washing dishes or a car, walking, or exercising) with keen, mindful awareness of the sensations that arise during the activity.

In the space provided, write which sensation most frequently grabs your attention, and why that one stands out.

Eating Meditation

In this session, you will be eating mindfully. This meditation can be done at home, a restaurant, a friend's house, or anywhere you eat. Place a dish of food in front of you and look at the food. Look at how the food is arranged on the plate. Look at each item of food individually. Look at the colors of the food. Notice how the food smells. Examine the food and appreciate every aspect you can perceive before you take a bite. Once you take a bite, truly taste the food and appreciate the taste.

REFLECTION

Write about your mindful eating experience in the space provided.

INTENTION

Today, I will truly experience all meals and snacks using all of my senses.

What do you think are the consequences of mindless eating? In the space provided, list the issues that are inherent in mindless eating.

This is the final set of the 22 meditations.
If you've gone through the journal in order,
these final meditations should help you hone
the skills you've been practicing for a while.
If you've been skipping around in the journal,
this set of meditations may seem a little more
challenging, but they should still be helpful!

Body Scan, Waking

This session will be a morning body scan. Upon waking, scan every part of your body you can manage to feel. Starting with your feet, feel the muscles and sinews as you flex and bend your feet; feel your ankles and calves. Try to focus on how you feel inside and out. Move your focus to your knees and thighs, flexing and bending your legs, and try to become aware of every molecule of your person. Notice any aches and pains. Move to your core, stomach, and back, then to your chest and shoulders. Zero in on every muscle, scanning each as slowly as you can. Focus on every bit of this experience. As you move on to your arms, hands, neck, and head, zoom in as far as you can and truly feel your body. Practice this meditation for 30 minutes. If you finish meditating before the time is up, begin again. Go as slowly as you can while still experiencing the body sensation.

REFLECTION

In the space provided, write about your experience of this session.

INTENTION

Today, I will examine every experience with laser focus.

How does performing a mindfulness practice session first thing in the morning affect your day?

Body Scan, Midday

This session will be a midday body scan. At this point, you've made it through your morning activities. Take some time in the middle of the day to observe how your body feels. Set aside 30 minutes to do a body scan like the waking one (see pages 16, 62, and 108). This time, try to use your growing focus to "zoom in" on each body part even further, like a microscope switching from 100x to 1,000x magnification. Starting with your feet, slowly go up your body to your head, and try to feel each muscle and joint as intimately as you can. Flex and relax each muscle, one at a time, while paying careful attention to every sensation.

REFLECTION

Once you've completed the session, reflect on your experience in the space provided.

INTENTION

Today, I will pay attention to my body and not overlook its sensations and needs.

Are you taking care of your body? In what ways could you improve your self-care regimen?

Body Scan, Bedtime

This will be a bedtime body scan. You will focus even more closely on your body than in previous sessions. While lying down, perform a body scan. This time, scan yourself more slowly and focus more intensely on every sensation and any aches and pains you have. Feel every muscle and joint from your feet all the way to your head. Flex and relax each muscle, one at a time, while maintaining mindfulness. Notice where each muscle begins and ends. Set a timer and practice this meditation for 30 minutes. If you complete the scan before the timer goes off, start again.

REFLECTION
Reflect on this session in the space provided.

INTENTION
Now that the day is over, I will attend to my body and let it relax.

What sensations do you notice in this "microscopic" focus that you weren't aware of before?

Mindful Journey

In this session, you will meditate on a time you had a long journey. This journey can be a road trip, a long hike, or a leisurely walk. Think of a long journey. Consider the travel experience and the new sights and sounds. Meditate on the experience of something new and stay here mentally for 30 minutes.

REFLECTION

Use the space provided to reflect on this travel session.

INTENTION

Today, I will travel somewhere new, and tune in to the sounds and sights around me, in order to fully experience the whole trip.

When traveling mindfully, what most grabs your attention?

Mindfulness of Emotions

Think of a significant emotional experience, one that felt all-consuming. Meditate on the chain of events that led to the peak of this experience. What pattern of events is there, if any? Did the experience result in some sort of outburst from you? Meditate on this experience for 30 minutes.

Reflect on your experience with this meditation in the space provided.

Today, I will observe my emotional state. As I do this activity, I will take a deep breath and examine the mental chain of events that have occurred before I react to a situation.

Examine the mental chain of events leading up to your emotional reaction to something. What patterns do you notice?

Impermanence in the Minute

Here's a meditation for the coffee lovers in the crowd. Prep your coffee, tea, or cocoa as you always do, but this time observe the impermanent loops and curls the creamer or milk creates as you pour it into the beverage. Let this inspire meditation on the impermanence of things. Whether you view impermanence as good or bad, nothing that has a beginning is without an end. Meditate on impermanence for 30 minutes.

REFLECTION

Reflect on your experience with this meditation in the space provided.

INTENTION

Today, I will focus on how common impermanence is in daily life.

What are some good and bad points to impermanence? List them.

Walking Meditation

This session is a walking meditation. You will focus intensely on the sensations you feel while you walk. Actively pay attention to feeling your feet strike the ground, and to how it feels to place weight on your feet and to pick them up and set them down. Witness the repetition. Focus on experiencing the entire walking exercise, utilizing all of your senses. Practice this meditation for 30 minutes.

REFLECTION

In the space provided, write about your experience performing a deep walking meditation.

INTENTION

Today, I will take a walk outside and consciously feel my steps.

Why is it that tasks that are repeated often are overlooked, and why don't we see the profound in the simple?

Contentment Meditation

In this meditation, we will focus on contentment. Look for the ways in which you are content and focus on the feeling of happiness. Practice this meditation for 30 minutes.

In the space provided, write about your experience exploring the sensation of contentment.

Today, I will focus on the ways in which I am content.

What defines your sense of contentment? What makes some people have more requirements and other people have fewer requirements to reach contentment?

Serenity Meditation

Find a reasonably quiet place. You can sit, stand, or walk. You can close your eyes or leave them half open. Half-open eyes are preferable if you are a little sleepy and can't nap. Also, half-opened eyes still allow for blinking. Bring your focus to your breath and the sensations of breathing. Concentrate either on the place where the breath enters and exits your body, or on the rise and fall sensation of the diaphragm. Focus on the most prominent sensation of the act of breathing. Continue this practice for 30 minutes.

REFLECTION

Reflect on your breathing meditation in the space provided.

INTENTION

Today, I will focus on my breathing and how it affects my emotional state.

What mental images arise when you meditate on your breath?

Gratitude Meditation

Gratitude is the state of being actively thankful for things and opportunities you have. Ponder an opportunity you are truly grateful for. Focus on this opportunity for 30 minutes. Consider all the subtleties of this opportunity.

Reflect on the effect this positive opportunity has had on your life.

Today, I will look for one thing for which I am truly grateful.

What things do you take for granted? What opportunities to practice gratitude are you missing?

Loving-Kindness Meditation, Self

This session will be a self-centered loving-kindness session, a style of meditation focusing on love and kindness. Stand, sit, or walk while envisioning yourself happy, healthy, safe, and cared for. If it helps, repeat the phrase "May I be happy, may I be healthy, may I be safe, may I be cared for." Maintain this practice for 30 minutes.

REFLECTION

Once you've completed your session, reflect on it briefly in the space provided.

INTENTION

Today, I will examine the source of my happiness.

What does happiness mean to you? What do you require to be happy?

Loving-Kindness Meditation, Neutral One

Continuing with loving-kindness, this session will center on a person you know of, or an acquaintance. This person should be someone you don't know well, and who inspires little emotional response from you. Choose someone you feel very neutral toward. Focus on this person. Imagine this person is happy, healthy, safe, and cared for. If it helps, you can softly repeat the phrase "May you be happy, may you be healthy, may you be safe, may you be cared for." Meditate on this person, in this way, for 30 minutes.

REFLECTION

Once you have completed this session, use the space provided to reflect on the experience of metta toward a person you are neutral about.

INTENTION

Today, I will genuinely consider the feelings of someone I don't know well.

What makes me invest mental energy in a person?

Loving-Kindness Meditation, Difficult One

Find a position of comfort and begin to imagine yourself happy, healthy, safe, and cared for. Then, just when you notice a tinge of positive emotions and you know the meditation is working, mentally swap the intended recipient of your positive thoughts. This time the lucky person is someone you don't like. Be brave and pick someone you really dislike. Imagine them happy, healthy, safe, and cared for. If it helps, you can softly repeat the phrase "May you be happy, may you be healthy, may you be safe, may you be cared for." This session may be tougher than the other loving-kindness sessions and may take longer to complete in earnest. Keep pushing through the exercise. Remember, this practice in no way condones or erases the past actions or behaviors of the person you are contemplating, and it won't give that person a pass to do wrong in the future. This exercise is about you releasing a grudge. Practice this meditation for at least 30 minutes.

REFLECTION

Reflect on your experience with this meditation in the space provided.

Consider what it would feel like to truly let go of all your grudges.

Why do you carry grudges?

Observing the Mind

In this meditation, you'll be practicing "mindfulness of the mind," in which you will use your mind to observe your mind. Find a position of comfort—sit, stand, or walk—and carefully observe your mind and your thoughts. Observe the mind and its ability to rise and fall (see pages 88 and 96). Practice this meditation for at least 30 minutes.

(see pages 88 and 96)

REFLECTION

Reflect on the effects of this practice in the space provided.

INTENTION

Today, I will observe my mind and where it's going hourly.

When you observe your mind, what thoughts regularly come up?

Random Act of Kindness Meditation

In this session, we will focus on a kind act and how it feels to perform it. This act can be big or small. Think about when you did something for someone else and focus on how doing it made you feel. Truly ruminate on this experience for 30 minutes.

Reflect on your experience with this meditation in the space provided.

Today, I will examine the motives behind my actions.

PROMPT

What does kindness mean to you?

Emptiness Meditation

In this session, you will be meditating on emptiness. Consider emptiness the most natural state of your mind. Generally speaking, we are at peace until something moves us from that neutral point. Focus on what your mind is doing when you aren't worried about school, work, bills, or any of the other things that trouble you. Examine this neutral space for 30 minutes.

REFLECTION

Use the space provided to reflect on this session.

INTENTION

Today, I will focus on the mental "quiet space" between my thoughts, without forcing thoughts out.

Where does your mind usually go from moment to moment?
What thoughts habitually stay on your mind?

Mantra Meditation

For this session, pick a mantra or affirmation to repeat. Choose something related to an issue you have. For instance, if you aren't feeling confident, try saying something like "I am worthy." Try to find a judgment-free area, somewhere you can get loud if you choose to, and spend 30 minutes reciting your mantra or affirmation. Put some power behind the recitation and focus on the vibrating quality of the sounds you're making.

REFLECTION

Write about your experience with this meditation in the space provided.

INTENTION

Today, I will focus on my inner dialogue.

Referring to your inner dialogue, what kinds of things are you "saying" in your mind?

Rise and Fall Meditation

Life consists of a steady cycle of natural ups and downs. Things tend to start, gradually increase, peak, and then decline. Everything in businesses and relationships, every action, comes about and falls away. Focus on the rise and fall sensations of your diaphragm, the muscle in the middle of your chest just below your rib cage, as you breathe. Fill your whole body with each breath and think or softly repeat to yourself "rise and fall." Practice this meditation for 30 minutes.

REFLECTION

Reflect on the rise and fall sensation of your breathing.

INTENTION

Today, I will notice other rise and fall patterns that I come across.

It has been said "the mind precedes all states of existence." Through the lens of rise and fall discussed earlier in the journal (see pages 88 and 96), what does this saying mean to you?

Mental "Quiet Space" Meditation

In this meditation, you will be looking at the mind and its processes. Get comfortable: sit, stand, or walk. Observe your mind. As soon as an active thought ends, focus on that quiet space. Apply your focus on the "space" between mental events. With repeated application, this space will expand. Once it does, you'll feel like you've built an addition onto your mind. Practice this meditation for 30 minutes.

REFLECTION

Write about your experience expanding the space between your thoughts in the space provided below.

INTENTION

Today, I will appreciate the open spaces in my life.

For many people, openness represents freedom. Do you agree?

Sadness Meditation

In this meditation, we will observe our mind in a moment of sadness. Think of a moment, big or small, when you felt sad. For many people, sadness can be a very engrossing emotional experience. Using your ever-sharpening awareness, observe the sad moment, focus on it, and examine it. What does thinking about this experience do to your state of mind? Practice this meditation for 30 minutes.

REFLECTION

Write about your experience meditating on sadness in the space provided.

INTENTION

Today, I will look for the "silver linings" present in a less-than-ideal moment.

When sadness arises, what do you think is the saddest part of it—
the event itself or your reaction to the event?

All-Sense Input Meditation

This meditation focuses on every experienced sensation. You are going to mentally track all your senses rather than focusing on one specific input. Use this session to work on broadening your meditative scope. Try to push the limits of what you perceive. Attempt to notice everything you see, hear, smell, and feel as you are carrying out your normal daily activities. Practice this meditation in 30-minute intervals throughout the day. Try the meditation more than once if you can.

REFLECTION

Reflect on your experience with this session in the space provided.

INTENTION

Today, I will challenge myself to actively experience what I do and appreciate how much is gained while I'm off "autopilot."

Why does your mind wander?

Last Meditation

This is the last meditation; you have now completed more than 65 separate sessions. Congratulations! In this session, flip back through the book and read over your reflections, intentions, and prompts.

Reflect on how far you've come in your practice in the space provided.

Today, I will assess the changes that meditation has brought to my life.

Over the course of these 66 meditations, how has your life changed?
How have you benefited from these meditations?

About the Author

Jim Martin is the lead creative behind TheUnusualBuddha.com. Jim lives in a small Virginia town with his wife of 15 years and three children. They are very supportive of his efforts—even if they are sometimes the source of how-to-be-mindful content inspiration. For two years, Jim regularly attended meditation classes with his teacher, Edward, who imparted many pieces of wisdom to Jim, one of which truly struck a chord. Edward said, "I don't teach students. I teach teachers." This inspired Jim to look for fresh ways to introduce people to meditation. It also inspired some deep thought around how meditation is taught and shared. Most efforts to spread those ideas seem to lack practical and realistic methods. Making meditation accessible and relatable has been a driving force for Jim's teaching and the inspiration behind his vlog, podcast, blog, and all the other attempts to get this simple life-changing advice into the hands of all who would seek it.